FOR ALL THE WRONG REASONS

Break through
Break down

Marriage
DESTINY OR DISTRUCTION

FOR ALL THE WRONG REASONS
MARRIAGE: DESTINY or DESTRUCTION
By: Erlease Freeman

Cover design by: Cecily Copes
Logo designs by: Andre M. Saunders
Editor: Eric Lose
Co-Editor: September Summers

© 2010 Erlease Freeman
ISBN 978-0-9843255-5-9/ISBN 0-9843255-5-7
Library of Congress Control Number: 2010925473

All Scripture references unless otherwise indicated are taken from the King James Version of the Bible. Scripture quotations marked KJV are taken from The Hebrew-Greek Key Study Bible King James Version © 1991 by AMG Publishers Chattanooga, Tennessee and from the Thompson Chain-Reference Bible 5th Improved Edition © 1988 by B. B. Kirkbride Bible Company, Inc. Indianapolis, Indiana.

Scripture quotations marked Today's NIV are taken from Today's New International Version © 2005 by Zondervan Corporation Grand Rapids, Michigan. Scripture quotations marked RSV are taken from The Revised Standard Version ©1962 by The World Publishing Company Cleveland, Ohio. All rights reserved. This book is protected under the copyright laws of the United States of America. This book may not be copied or reprinted for commercial gain or profit. The use of short quotations or occasional page copying for personal or group study is permitted and encouraged. Permission will be granted on request. For Worldwide Distribution. Printed in the United States of America. Published by Jazzy Kitty Greetings Marketing & Publishing, LLC dba Jazzy Kitty Publishing. Using Microsoft Publishing Software.

ACKNOWLEDGMENTS

To Elder Artensa Snow (Tabernacle of Praise Worship Church, Chester, PA) "It all started with you."

To Valerie Coleman (Pen of the Writer, Dayton, OH) "For the workshop where this project was birthed."

To Eric Lose (Cincinnati, OH) "Editor extraordinaire."

To Co-Pastor Velva J. Rainey (New Antioch FGBC, Newark, DE) "Thank you for sharing your years of experience and wisdom."

To Missionary Nadine Collins (Canaan Baptist Church) "Thank you for the referral."

To Evangelist Anelda Attaway (Jazzy Kitty Greetings Marketing and Publishing, Wilmington, DE) "Words could never express..."

To Lil' Cec "Continue to let God use you for His glory; He's got great things in store for you. Don't give up on Him."

To Prophetess Francine Riley (Atlanta, GA) "The prophecy has come to pass." (Englewood, OH July 2006)

To First Lady Pamela Maddox (Englewood, OH) "What a Conference... What a move of God; I'll never forget."

...and to all who will buy and read this book (May you be blessed).

DEDICATION

To my first husband: "the Lord of hosts is his name;" my Redeemer, "Holy One of Israel;" (Isaiah 54:5). You rejoice over me as a bridegroom rejoices over his bride (Isaiah 62:5); you have promised never to leave me, nor forsake me (Hebrews 13:5). You loved me first; you love me best.

*In an effort to give the enemy no acknowledgment, the author has chosen not to capitalize the first letter of his name throughout this manuscript, and request that you ignore the improper English [rule] except at the beginning of a sentence.

TABLE OF CONTENTS

Foreword i
   Chapter 1: S-E-X Does Not Spell Love 01
   Chapter 2: Addicted 08
   Chapter:3: A Time for Warfare 14
   Chapter 4: Money, Money, Money 20
   Chapter 5: Learning to Trust GOD Again 24
   Chapter 6: Destiny 27
   Chapter:7: Is it Real? 31
   Chapter 8: Called to Be 37
   Chapter 9: Basic Training 44
   Chapter 10: He Loves Me, He Loves Me Not 48
   Chapter:11: Alone, But Not Lonely 55
   Chapter 12: Still Not Delivered 62
   Chapter 13: Don't Be Discouraged 66
   Chapter 14: Walk the Walk 69
   Chapter 15: Prepare to be Found 74
   Chapter 16: Now that I'm Found 77
References 83
Elder Velva J. Rainey, Co-Pastor... 84
About the Author 85

FOREWORD

"For All the Wrong Reasons" appears to be the book of choice 'For All the Right Reasons'. The author has sought to weave a tapestry of self-propelled scenarios with that of basic Bible knowledge to assist the reader as well as one that directs us to a personal look into her own life and one of self-examination of our own. From the titles written in the Table of Contents, before ever reading a single chapter's line, the reader will be led into an array of "life-lived" possibilities. As with similar titles, one might be able to place themselves in their own "life-lived" scenario. And, yes, we would have found ourselves there 'for all the wrong reasons'. But because of words like "destiny", and "called", and "trust in God", we can "walk the walk" and possibly be "alone but not lonely".

From the perspective of one who has been married for more than 25 years, I am able to see how someone could get caught up in the plight to find oneself married. That is if the persons to whom you associate with are married and appear insanely happy! Then, of course, others would want to experience that unconditional love which brings that couple so much joy and happiness. But, for many seekers of the "I do" response or the "will you" question... they are seeking, as the author states..."For All the Wrong Reasons".

How many times have you stopped to take a look inward? When was the last time you evaluated your relationships? Why they worked or didn't work? This author takes you on a journey and gives a birds-eye view into her own reflection of her relationships. And oddly enough, they were not all 'husband-wife' relationship views. But, a general look at how we, as individuals, respond to others based on our own personal flaws. We should not be looking to another person to fulfill us. Then we would be able to find a complementary relationship that would add to our own pre-existing joy as an individual.

At what point do we listen to an "All-Mighty, All-Knowing God" as opposed to the advice of a friend or acquaintance who only knows as much as you've told them. It is at those moments in our lives that we should take a step back and review our previous outcomes. How can decisions made now change the way we interact with others in our relationships? What adjustments can we make in our own personal lives that may affect how we seek to engage ourselves in relationships? How accepting do you really have to be of someone else's opinion of you? The sooner we learn that we are placed on this earth to bring Glory to God and His handiwork... the better off we'd be! Think about it... how can someone tell you that you're undeserving of love, or you'll never amount to anything, or that you're worthless, when the Word of God clearly lets us know that "God so loved the world that He gave..." (John 3:16). And why would an "All-Mighty, All-Knowing God" waste His time on you and me if we were undeserving of His love, or worthless? I dare say that it is 'For All the Right Reasons' that He loves us and wants us to love Him in return. But, instead, we choose everyone and everything other than Him, and His Son- Jesus, "For All the Wrong Reasons".

If we would slow down when reading 1 Corinthians 13, when it says "Love is patient..." and stop there! Be patient and wait on the Lord! Not only will He love you unconditionally, but He will give you the desires of your heart. We must remember that the first part of our self-examination is to recall that we need to do a (paraphrased Matthew 6:33) 'seek first the Kingdom of God-then all other things will be added unto us', then we won't be involved in relationships for all the wrong reasons... but rather for all the right reasons. Know your limits; know what tempts you; so that when that temptation comes you can resist it. Realize your destiny and who you were called to be by the Creator; know He will teach you, and lead you into all truth. Above all else, know that He loves you – when it seems that no one else does, or that there is no one there, remember His word says that "he would never leave us nor forsake us". And that's probably more than anyone can promise in any relationship these days. But Gods promises are true; and He is a God that cannot lie. So challenge yourself – take a good look at yourself. The greatest change you can experience is the one that you create. Are you in a relationship of Destiny or Destruction?

CHAPTER 1

S- E- X Does Not Spell Love

Sex, sex, and more sex! Surely, it must be unhealthy to think about sex so much. Instead of meditating on the Word of God as Psalm 1:2(b) says, my mind was stayed on getting my flesh satisfied. This was my number one reason for getting married- LEGAL SEX. I could have all the sex I wanted, when I wanted, and would not have to wake up the next morning and repent.

Marriage, the Bible says "...is honorable in all, and the bed undefiled:" (Hebrews 13:4(a) KJV). The Greek word for undefiled, *amiantos* signifies unpolluted or unfading. But many of us have polluted marriage by twisting the Word of God for our own purposes. Marriage is supposed to be unfading. Marriage is supposed to last forever. Remember when we took our vows? We (those of us who have been married) said "for better or for worse... in sickness and in health... forsaking all others... as long as we both shall live..." But we really did not mean that. What we really meant was "...as long as everything is going well... as long as all of my bills are paid and I do not have to struggle... as long as he is not getting on my nerves... as long as she can cook... as long as she does not have a headache every night...".

One man after another, one woman after another, relationship after relationship—the number one question in the hearts and on the minds of many is: "if I sex you will you love me?" Whether it was a father who was not there, a mother who walked out, or an uncle who abused us sexually, there were many issues in our pasts that caused us to think no one loved us.

These negative thoughts pushed us (men and women) into the arms, and the beds of others thinking: "all I want is someone to love me". Women think that if they sex a man good enough he will love them; if he does not tell them he loves them, they will sex him again... and again. Better the next time, longer, different; whatever it takes. Women feel they have to try to make a man love them because they did not receive that love as a child. After all is said and done, and the relationship ends (no, not relationship... affair), these men leave women feeling like prostitutes: prostitutes who did not even get paid.

Why do women continue to allow men to abuse [abnormally use] them? Experience tells us that these ungodly relationships do not last, but many feel as though they cannot live alone; we think: "I need a man in my life" or "I need a woman in my life", as if to say that when God created us He created us broken. Loneliness, fear, low self-esteem, and feelings of inadequacy have caused many to think that being single and/or being alone was taboo. So we move on to the next prospect—someone else to trap; someone else who may love us since the last one did not. All along collecting loads and loads of baggage; and if by some slim chance we did encounter someone who really loved us we would not even realize it because we are so messed up emotionally.

Many of us do not even recognize nor can we appreciate *real* love. Because we do not know what real love is, we end up doing something to sabotage our relationships; whether consciously or subconsciously, intentionally or unintentionally we find a way to chase our partners into the arms and beds of someone else. Love was like an alien to me—foreign; and so it made me feel uncomfortable.

Many of you may be able to relate to a life that is like a merry-go-round; going around and around in circles—dizzy, and all messed up. First John 4:7-8 says "Beloved, let us love one another: for love is of God; and every one that loveth is born of God, and knoweth God. He that loveth not knoweth not God; for God is love." (KJV) Before we are born again the love of God is not in us; and so it is that we are unable to give and/or experience real love—the God kind of love. The first time I experienced true love in my life was in 1996. This man of God told me that he loved me like he loved his own body. I had no clue what he was talking about—but it sounded good; and so I married him. I later learned that Ephesians exhorts men "...to love their wives as their own bodies." (Ephesians 5:28a KJV) This man really loved me—and I knew it not.

Did my father really love me? How come he never told me? Maybe he did not know how to show and tell—maybe no one ever showed him or told him. The wise man that he is, told me many things; but I do not remember him ever telling me as a child nor in my teenage years that he loved me. Emotional scars of self-hate were formed very early. I recall sometime in my 20's asking him: "How come you never tell me that you love me, or that you are proud of me?" His response still resounds in my mind today..."I love you" he said, "and I am proud of you". But it was not convincing enough for me to believe it; it was said in a very sarcastic tone, and became like mere words with no substance. And so I continued to search for someone or something that would make me *feel* love. In all of my searching, I could find no drug, no partner, nor alcoholic beverage that would fulfill.

The Bible says "But if they cannot contain, let them marry: for it is better to marry than to burn." (I Corinthians 7:9 KJV) Sex seems like a good reason to get married; after all we do want to live right, don't we? Some think that there is safety in marriage. We stand on the scripture that says "Nevertheless, to avoid fornication, let every man have his own wife, and let every woman have her own husband." (I Corinthians 7:2 KJV)

The issue, however, is that immoral sex is more than just fornication. Pornography, prostitution, masturbation, lust, adultery, lesbianism, homosexuality, and even abortion all constitute immoral sexual sin. Abortion, you might ask; yes, abortion. Abortion is a way to cover up the results of repeated immoral sexual sin. Immoral includes anything contrary to moral principles. Synonymous with immoral is wicked, depraved, corrupt, dissolute, dishonest, dissipated, decadent, debauched, sinful, and iniquitous. Iniquitous is any behavior that is utterly harmful and wrong; especially in a way that results in great injustice or unfairness.

Now we may think that masturbation and pornography do not qualify as iniquitous because they are not unjust or unfair acts; we may think that our participation and/or practice of these acts do not affect others. We must realize, however, that spirits attach themselves as we practice these acts and result in behaviors that do negatively impact others whom we are in relationships with or with whom we may become involved.

David said in Psalm 51:5 "Behold, I was shapen in iniquity; and in sin did my mother conceive me." (KJV) Psalm 51 is a Penitent Psalm. It is David's prayer for remission of his sin with Bathsheba. You see, David was "...a man after God's own heart..." (Acts 13:22 KJV), but David had 'issues'. David—like many of us—had issues in his flesh. Now to say that you have issues in your flesh, in and of itself does not present a problem; the problem comes when we do not know how to crucify our flesh. Galatians 5:24 tells us "And they that are Christ's have crucified the flesh with the affections and lusts." (KJV) The word crucify in this context comes from a Greek word that implies we are to mortify our affections and lusts through the faith and love of the crucified Christ.

The Bible says that David looked upon a woman one day and lusted after her. Not only did he lust after her, but he made a decision that he was going to pursue her. We must realize that sin is a choice. David made a choice to pursue Bathsheba and ended up having an adulterous affair with her. Remember, Bathsheba was married—to a man named Uriah (read II Samuel chapter 11). After David committed adultery with Bathsheba he plotted murder to cover up his sin. When Nathan the prophet came to David in II Samuel chapter 12, David did not realize that the Lord had exposed his sin. He told the man of God "...As the Lord liveth, the man that hath done this thing shall surely die: And he shall restore the lamb fourfold, because he did this thing, and because he had no pity." (II Samuel 12:5b-6 KJV). We must also realize that God sees and He knows everything. The Bible says "...and be sure your sin will find you out" (Numbers 32:23b KJV). I have heard it said that God can see a black ant in a black hole on a black night.

Not only does God see our sin when we think that no one else does, but he is also a righteous judge. Scripture tells us that judgment was served on David and his house—evil was raised up right in King David's home. The king's wives would be taken from him and given to others. David's sin was done in secret, but the judgment of God was going to be open for all to see (cf II Samuel chapters 12 and 13; II Samuel 16:20-23). James 1:15 says "Then when lust hath conceived, it bringeth forth sin: and sin, when it is finished, bringeth forth death." (KJV) The word of God is still true—you do reap what you sow.

As we continue to read the story we see that David made the same mistake that many of us make today; he married the woman because she was pregnant. The Bible does not tell us that David sought the Lord for his wife, nor does it tell us that the prophet spoke to David and told him that Bathsheba was supposed to be his wife. It does not even detail a dating experience between David and Bathsheba giving them time to get to know one another. David, like many of us, just wanted what he wanted, and he wanted it when he wanted it.

I encourage you to consider thoroughly marrying someone for the sake of giving a baby a name. Man makes mistakes; God does not make mistakes. There is no law that says that you must marry because you are pregnant or have gotten someone pregnant. If pregnancy is your only reason for wanting to marry and you do not hear the spirit of God calling you to that, then do not consider that as an option. It is imperative, however, that both individuals repent, ask God for forgiveness, and then dedicate the baby to the Lord. The baby will have a name; his/her name will be "CHILD OF GOD". Remember, as previously stated, we are mortal beings and are subject to mistakes; God, however, is not human. He does not make mistakes. The Word tells us in Isaiah 55:8 that His thoughts are not our thoughts, and that his ways are much higher than our ways.

Even though David repented for his sin, he still had to suffer the consequences because of the choices he made—and we do too. We suffer many consequences because of our choices that we make in life. Although we cannot go back and change anything, we can pray for God's grace to get us through the rough times that we may go through due to the choices we have made in life.

CHAPTER 2
Addicted

I woke up one morning after about six months of marriage, and realized that I did not really *like* my husband. I had married him 'for all the wrong reasons'. He qualified based on his salvation. But that was not enough to keep me in my marriage. I was uninformed and inexperienced; I had no knowledge, skills, or understanding to qualify me for the covenant of marriage. Additionally, I'd had no pre-marital counseling.

The Bible says "...What therefore God hath joined together, let not man put asunder." (Matthew 19:6b KJV). We must realize that every union is not God joined. It is also possible, however, that God ordained the union, but for a different time or season. Do you know anyone who was married, divorced, and then remarried-to the same person? God is so awesome. He is able to mend broken hearts and broken marriages. If God ordained a man and a woman to be together, they will be together-in His time and in His season-to fulfill His purposes. Keep in mind that everything that we, as Christians, say, think, and do is ultimately going to affect and/or impact the kingdom of God; remember his ways and thoughts are higher than our ways and thoughts. He has a plan.

Almost 30 years ago I was involved in a relationship where I thought that this man loved me; I also thought that I loved him. Needless to say my heart was crushed. As I reflect on those years of my life, however, I cannot blame that man for breaking my heart. Because our hearts were not yielded first to God, we could not experience true love. We were destined to fail and to break each others hearts. Keep in mind that men and women alike are subject to a broken heart.

That hurt that I experienced during those tender years of 'woman-hood' opened up the door to another generational curse—*adultery*. I began to find [what I thought was] safety in adulterous affairs. I made a vow to myself that I would never give my heart to another man; I reasoned within myself that I could use men to get my (physical) needs fulfilled, and that I would never have to give my heart completely, thereby avoiding heartbreak. After many years, however, I began to realize just how empty my life really was, and that I was truly unfulfilled. After the climax there was nothing; I was broken, frustrated, and devoid of love. By this time in my life I had unknowingly attracted many spirits; the main two spirits being a spirit of adultery, and a spirit of lust. Ultimately, the only men who were drawn to me were married men. I attracted countless men with only one motive—to use me for their pleasure and then discard me as trash. Because I did not love myself I allowed this for many years.

Proverbs says, "Wisdom will save you from the ways of wicked men, from men whose words are perverse," (2:12). Verses 16-17 of that same chapter says "...it will save you also from the adulteress, from the wayward wife with her seductive words, who has left the partner of her youth and ignored the covenant she made before God." (NIV) Beware women. Your search for love could result in a whole lot of other issues that you may not be prepared to deal with in life. It may lead you somewhere you do not want to be. When you turn around to try to find your way back the bridge behind you may be collapsed; all other roads may be closed. The fog will be so thick (in your mind) that the only way for you to go is forward; forward into further destruction.

Western Medieval legend has it that there are demons—one named incubus and one named succubus. Based on the scripture in Genesis the sixth chapter, it is believed that the male demon incubus lies upon women, and the female demon succubus goes into men while they are sleeping. These demons are believed to have sexual intercourse with humans, causing a preoccupation with sin, especially sexual sin.

Do you ever wonder why you wake up *wet*, or feeling extra *horny*? There may come a time when you will be 'addicted' to sex. Now why does that sound so strange to you? We hear of alcoholics, and drug addicts, but did you know that you could be a sex addict... a sexaholic? Webster's defines *nymphomania* as an "abnormal, uncontrollable sexual desire in a female" and *satyriasis* as an "abnormal, uncontrollable sexual desire in a male." Incubus comes from the Latin word incubare, which means to lie upon; succubus comes from the Latin word succuba which means prostitute. They cause such a preoccupation so that all an individual can think about is sex. Genesis 6:1-4 reads "And it came to pass, when men began to multiply on the face of the earth, and daughters were born unto them, that the sons of God saw the daughters of men that they were fair; and they took them wives of all which they chose. And the Lord said, My spirit shall not always strive with man, for that he also is flesh: yet his days shall be a hundred and twenty" (KJV)

The Bible speaks of 'giants' in the earth during those times. When the sons of God [came in unto] had intercourse with the daughters of men they bare offspring that were unholy; these 'sons of God' are believed to be Incubus and Succubus. Years later, their offspring are still being multiplied upon the earth.

It is not uncommon that sex addicts have experienced some sort of emotional or sexual trauma in their childhood. Some behaviors which may be indicative of sexual addiction include: soliciting prostitutes (male and/or female); sacrificing money meant for bills (rent/mortgage, utilities, food, and clothing) and using it instead to obtain sexual favors (legal and/or illegal); overspending on Playboy and/or other sex related literature; over obsession with sexual toys; repeated adulterous affairs; inability to be satisfied no matter how much sex you get; inability to be satisfied no matter how many partners you may have; more than one sexual partner at the same time; and spending countless hours on the internet or telephone having internet sex or phone sex. These are just a few behaviors that should cause you to think that you may have a problem in this area.

II Corinthians 13:5 tells us to examine ourselves; it reads "Examine yourselves, whether ye be in the faith; prove your own selves. Know ye not your own selves, how that Jesus Christ is in you, except ye be reprobates?" (KJV) When you examine yourself in this sense, you are discovering what good and what evil lies within; what weaknesses and strengths you possess. If you judge yourself, you will not have to be concerned with someone else judging you. When you lay on your face before the Lord He will begin to show you everything within that is not like Him; He will help you to discern what needs to be burned out and/or taken away. It does not feel good, but it is a necessary process. Just as gold needs to go through a process in order to be purified, we as Christians need to go through a process also to purify us and make us more like Jesus (read Zechariah 13:9, and I Peter 1:7).

Many times in relationships, we tell people that we love them; but do we really know what love is? As stated previously, God is love; and if we do not love ourselves, we cannot possibly love another person. I recall a minister once encouraging me to look in the mirror and begin to tell myself that I loved me; this was supposed to begin some sort of healing and/or therapy of sorts. When I went home, I attempted to do as I was instructed. As I looked at myself in the mirror I began to cry–uncontrollably; I saw the image looking back at me and was filled with anger, hate, and even rage. I hated what I saw–I hated who I had become; I was angry because I had allowed the enemy to turn me into someone (some 'thing') that could not please God. It was also hard for me to believe that God could really love someone like me; that He could [or would] ever forgive me for the horrible life I had lived. I am not just talking about before salvation–I am speaking of my life after salvation as well.

Christians, it is time for us to get right! Stop taking advantage of God's grace. Jesus is soon to come. We do not have much time left to *get* ready; we need to *be* ready. I told the Lord (and myself) one day I am tired of all the jumping and shouting in church, and when my feet touch the ground I am not able even to walk upright before

God. We must get tired of the enemy playing ping-pong (if you will) with our minds. It becomes like a game of soccer; the field portraying our lives and the enemies back and forth with the ball (our minds) playing untiringly until one of them wins.

CHAPTER 3

A Time for Warfare

If you believe that this is an area in which you need help, seek God earnestly. He is "...able to do exceeding abundantly above all that we ask or think, according to the power that worketh in us." (Ephesians 3:20 KJV) I strongly encourage you to be consistent and persistent in praying and fasting. Seek God continually for deliverance in this area of your life (1 Thessalonians 5:17). The enemy will not willingly let you go. John 10:10 says, "The thief comes only to steal and kill and destroy" (Today's NIV). Matthew 11:12 says "And from the days of John the Baptist until now the kingdom of heaven suffereth violence, and the violent take it by force." (KJV) A sister in Christ used to tell me repeatedly, 'when you get mad enough at the devil, it will not be a problem for you to live right'. You have to not only be serious about your deliverance, but you must be violent; you have to be determined that you are going to get back everything (joy, peace of mind, self-respect) that the enemy has stolen from you.

Before you go to sleep at night, pray for peace in your sleep. Pray against the enemies that will come to you in your sleep—in your dreams—and rob you of your strength. Sexual addiction, like all other addictions, is a compulsion that leaves you with an unmanageable nature. Read Matthew 16:19, Matthew 18:18, II Corinthians 10:4-6, Psalm 16:7-9, Psalm 127:2, and Proverbs 3:24. Be specific in your prayers. No one knows what you are going through or what you are experiencing better than you. Do not play with the enemy—the enemy is not playing with you. Satan has only one plan for your life; death, destruction, and everlasting torment in a burning hell (read John 10:10).

To say that it is important for a man and woman to discuss sex in pre-marital counseling is an understatement; it is essential. You must be open and honest with your intended spouse about past relationships, past experiences, sexual desires, expectations, etc. I am not saying to share everything you have done in your past [our past is covered under the blood of Jesus], but I do encourage you to share—as you are led by the Holy Spirit. We must be very sure before we take that long walk down the aisle... before we spend those hundreds and thousands of dollars that we have complete and total deliverance in all areas. It will be well worth it for you to push your wedding date back if you feel that you need more time. I am sure that your fiancé wants you to be whole; I am sure that he/she will understand. If this union is truly of God, they should be more than willing to go through any counseling with you to assure that you reach that level in God where He is calling you to be in your marriage, and in your life.

The Bible says in Luke 11:24-26 "When the unclean spirit is gone out of a man, he walketh through dry places, seeking rest; and finding none, he saith, I will return unto my house whence I came out. And when he cometh, he findeth it swept and garnished. Then goeth he, and taketh to him seven other spirits more wicked than himself; and they enter in, and dwell there: and the last state of that man is worse than the first." (KJV) You see, these demons will try to come back and haunt you in your marriage; if you allow that then you will be doomed for destruction.

Before you say "I do" to another human being, make sure to tell God "I do". Tell God, "I do love you first." Tell Him, "God I do want to live holy". Tell God, "I do want to please you first". Finally, tell God "I do want to fulfill my destiny in you". Ask God to help you remain faithful to your spouse; ask Him to show you what your destiny and your purpose is. Amos 3:3 asks the question "Can two walk together, except they be agreed?" (KJV) Have some prayer warriors come into agreement with you about your plans to marry. Connect with other married couples who are standing and believing God; couples who know the fight, and are willing to touch and agree with you.

You can make a decision to live holy as a single person as you wait for God to send you a mate. You can be delivered in your marriage if you have gotten off track. Galatians 2:20 says "I am crucified with Christ..." You must be willing to kill your flesh. As stated earlier, sin is a choice. You can tell the devil, 'NO'. It is not about me; it is not about you. It is about God. Time spent fasting and praying–time spent in private with God will burn up everything that is not like Him.

I wish to offer this prayer to all who are willing to surrender their lives and tell God, 'YES':

Father, I pray right now for every single woman and every single man who has a desire to please you. Keep them, according to your word in Jude 24. Teach them to oil their faith according to Jude 20. I pray for every man and every woman who has been bound by an adulterous spirit. I pray for deliverance right now in the name of Jesus. Satan, I command you to loose them and let them go! As they surrender and submit their will to you God, and as they spend time in secret prayer and worship; as they actively and consciously crucify their flesh, Father, I pray that you let your strength be made perfect in their weakness. I pray for the person who is reading right now who thinks this is an impossible thing. I pray right now for that woman who is not ready to let go. I pray God that you would sever every soul tie. I come against every generational curse in the name of Jesus. Let the blood of Jesus rush to every place in their lives where healing balm is needed. Father I pray for every marriage that has been negatively impacted by immoral sin. I pray for the wives, that you would comfort them. I pray for the husbands, that you would heal them in their emotions. I come against divorce in the name of Jesus. Father, you are able to do exceeding abundantly above all that we could ever ask or think, and I believe you right now for complete and total healing and deliverance in this area, for your people. In the name of Jesus I pray–AMEN.

Child of God, once you receive this prayer into your spirit, read the Word in Galatians 5:1 and Romans 8:1 to encourage yourself. God does hear and answer prayer if we just believe.

You can have a love affair with Jesus and He will not just 'wear you out' in your flesh. You can experience His limitless love if you desire. He will love you until you become whole and complete. He will minister to you as no other human being ever has or ever will. He will love your spirit, your mind, your body, and your emotions.

God takes great pleasure in us. He tells us in His Word how beautiful we are; not just on the outside, but on the inside (read Psalm 139:14-18). He will rock you; He will comfort you. God will satisfy you in areas where you never thought you could be satisfied.

Pamper yourselves ladies; go out and buy yourselves some flowers. Buy yourselves diamonds and furs. Shop at Victoria's Secret™; get massages. Treat yourselves to a manicure, a pedicure, and a facial; you may even want to get a full body spa treatment. Allow Jesus to be your man. We should look, *and* smell beautiful for Him; free of the *aroma* of sin. More than that, we should 'be' beautiful for Him; Holy and without blemish. Jesus deserves the best of all of us. We should never give Him less than we would give any other man in our lives.

The enemy constantly attacked me in my mind telling me that I would not have a life if I surrendered to Christ. "You won't have any fun"..."you will be lonely"..."you will be bored"..."no one wants to hang out with a *holy roller*"... and "you will surely lose that man". But the Holy Spirit ministered to me one morning in prayer and allowed me to realize that yes, I am crucified with Christ; yes, I am dead. My life as I knew it was over. He allowed me to realize that it was not about me. Nevertheless, as I lived my life (in my flesh) I was living by faith in the Son of God. I had to learn to trust and depend completely on Christ because He loved me, and had given himself completely for me. He had made the ultimate sacrifice for me (Based on Galatians 2:20).

Even with all the tests and trials that we go through in life, we can still have the time of our lives. I am living my best life right now, because I am living my life with purpose. Struggles do not seem as tough; God will bring you through and He will bring you out every time. "Now thanks be unto God, which always causeth us to triumph in Christ" (II Corinthians 2:14 KJV).

CHAPTER 4
Money, Money, Money

My second reason for getting married was to receive help paying my bills. When it came to money, too often it seemed there was never enough. Basic necessities were too much to handle alone. Child support payments were so inconsistent. Friends and family would open their doors to me when I was in need of shelter; but as a single parent with only one child, I felt I should have been doing better.

My level of income added to my embarrassment. I knew people who made less money, had more children, and were doing better than I. My pride would not allow me to apply for welfare. I believed in working hard for whatever I wanted, not depending on anyone for a handout. I had been working since the age of 14, and was always blessed with good jobs. I reasoned in my mind that I was 'too good' for welfare. No matter how hard I worked, however, there always seemed to be 'more month at the end of my money'.

How many of you have endured abusive relationships because you were *afraid* to leave? We were afraid not only for our safety, but we were afraid that we would not be able to survive (financially) without the abuser's help. God, however, is a faithful God. When we do finally get up the nerve to leave, He will send people to help and to bless us. I recall many years working full-time at night and going to school full-time during the day in order to obtain my degree. A very dear friend kept my daughter for me and did not charge me for childcare. More than emotional support, she was my greatest [human] source of spiritual support and encouragement. My daughter often told us she did not get saved in church; *"...I got saved right in my Aunt Bev's house".*

One of my favorite scriptures can be found in Psalm 119:7. It reads: "It is good for me that I have been afflicted; that I might learn thy statutes" (KJV). Andre Crouch sang a song years ago, 'If I never had a problem I would never know that God could solve them—I would never know what faith in His word could do'. I can attest to the fact that through all I have been through, I have learned to trust in God for myself. No matter what you are going through stay in church; no matter how great a sin you have committed, do not leave God. You may feel empty and feel that you are miles away from God; but there is safety within the walls of the church. Your deliverance is just one word away. Stay in the church.

As I look back on the years before I got married, I recall I had no savings, did not own a home, had mounds of debt, and nothing to bring to the table. Nothing, that is, but baggage; baggage from past relationships and past hurts. My ex-husband and I were two young people in love (so we thought) wanting to 'live right'. We chose to marry without receiving pre-marital counseling; we chose to marry without the blessing of our parents and/or our pastors. We soon discovered the common difficulties that married couples encounter. Our number one struggle became finances.

Single parents, no matter how good you think you may be doing by yourself, a little help is better than no help at all. However, 'help paying the bills' is not [in and of itself] good enough reason to marry. Marriage can be difficult. If your main reason for wanting to get married falls into this category, you should quickly reconsider. If you have gotten married already, and are having difficulty adjusting, you can still seek Godly counsel. Although the enemy may try to discourage you, causing you to waver in your faith, continue to trust God. Satan does not want to see you prospering in any way. He hates unity.

The Bible says, "Two are better than one, because they have a good return for their labor" (Ecclesiastes 4:9 Today's NIV). Even though out of season, you can still believe God to work a plan for your good. Do not permit the enemy to disrupt your destiny because of finances; because you may not have everything that you want. No one wants to struggle, however, God did promise to supply our needs—not our wants.

We must understand that marriage requires an adjustment period; some say three years, some say five years, some say seven years. However long the adjustment period may be, the joining together of two individual lives requires work. Marriage is not a game. Pray with and for your spouse; believe that God will see you through.

The Bible says, "But seek ye first the kingdom of God, and his righteousness; and all these things shall be added unto you." (Matthew 6:33 KJV) What are the '…all these things…'? Verse 31 of that same chapter reads, "Therefore take not thought, saying, What shall we eat? or, What shall we drink? or, Wherewithal shall we be clothed?" (KJV) God knows our needs and He has promised to provide for our needs. How is it that God has worked so many miracles in our pasts, yet we continue to allow the enemy to consume our minds with doubt, worry, and fear? Women, we cannot allow the enemy to drive us from our position of 'helpmate'. We must choose not to step out of position and continue to help our spouses no matter how difficult things become.

The Bible says "Where no counsel is, the people fall: but in the multitude of counselors there is safety" (Proverbs 11:14 KJV). Seek out a financial adviser if you must; it will pay off in the end. Jones and Bartlett Publishers define wisdom as: "...the ability to apply valuable and viable knowledge, experience, understanding, and insight while being prudent and sensible..." Godly counsel, both in marriage *and* in finances is sound wisdom.

CHAPTER 5

Learning to Trust GOD Again

Single mothers, it is not easy, but we can get to the place where we do not *need* a man to help pay our bills. Although we may have someone we can call if we need help, there will always be a price to pay. It may be an unspoken request; but women we know when someone is trying to get us to fulfill an obligation. We must make up our minds that we will live holy no matter the cost.

I recall years where I had overextended myself financially after God had brought me through. We were finally living 'the good life' [or so I thought]. When times got real hard, however, I would have to make a decision not to look back and call [that old friend] for help. My bills would get paid, but the ultimate cost would be more than I was willing to pay.

I recall being sent home from work due to overstaffing. I also recall being without a pay check for weeks at a time while in between jobs. I have taken cuts in pay so that I could devote more time to the work of the ministry. I have given tithes and offerings, knowing full well that I could have utilized that money to pay a bill.

There may come a time in our lives when God will challenge us. God wants to know if we really trust him. I wrote a book "El Shaddai–God My Sufficiency" (Rivers of Living Water Publishing, 2006). Although I had written the book, God began to challenge me as to whether I truly believed what I had written. Was my trust really in God when the pay check was not there, or had I began to put my trust in man?

El Shaddai is translated: *The All-Sufficient One; the God of the mountains; God Almighty. God is the all-sufficient source of all of our blessings; God is all-powerful; our problems are not too big for God to handle.* My mentor instructed me one day to, "...go back and read your own book." Somewhere along the way I began to loose hope. Although I knew that God was able to do anything, I began to wonder if He *wanted* to do for me what I desired him to do. Was my will truly aligned with His?

God showed me in Judges 7:2, that lest I, like the Israelites, say my own hand has saved me, I had to be humbled. You see, the Israelites had been delivered out of Egypt and ended up wandering in the wilderness for 40 years. I equate my life to Israel wandering in the wilderness for 40 years. Deuteronomy Chapter 8 exhorts me to obedience because of God's mercy and goodness to me. The purpose of my 40-year wilderness wandering was to humble me–to test me so that God would know my heart. The benefits of my obedience and surrendered life have been simply awesome. God has to always keep me reminded that "...it is he that giveth thee power to get wealth, that he may establish his covenant..." (Deut 8:18 KJV). We have a promise my friends recorded in the Word of God in Mark 10:29-30. God is going to re-pay us for everything that we have had to give up.

It is not easy to stand when you are faced with eviction making $80,000 per year. Because I was mismanaging money, and making wrong choices, I had found myself in a dilemma. I was moving my vehicle from week to week trying to keep the finance company from finding it until I could get caught up. I was working overtime on top of overtime trying to make ways; burning myself out, missing church, and not paying my tithes. I almost found myself getting married again just so that I could have help. I have said before, we cannot go back and change the past, but if we repent, God is able to get us back into alignment with His will for our lives.

In the midst of all that God had brought me through I have learned a valuable lesson. We cannot help others if we have not gone through something ourselves. We must 'come out' in order to minister to someone else that God is able to bring them out.

My friend, make up your mind not to compromise. Single ladies, you may be involved with a man who you feel really loves you. You may be praying that he will get himself together so that the two of you can marry. As long as you continue to compromise, however, he will not marry you. My father used to tell me, "he ain't gonna buy the cow, if he can get the milk for free." Ladies, we must stop giving away *free milk*. The Bible says: "What! Know ye not that your body is the temple of the Holy Ghost which is in you, which ye have of God, and ye are not your own? For ye are bought with a price: therefore glorify God in your body, and in your spirit, which are God's." (1 Corinthians 6:19-20 KJV).

The Greek word for glorify is *doxazo*, which means to recognize, to honor, and to praise. Recognize that you are worth more than some cheap thrill; begin to honor yourself as God honors you. We are of such value to God. When we reach that realization, we can worship Him the way he wants to be worshiped—in Spirit and in truth (John 4:23-24). Ladies, let us learn to trust God again; trust Him to bring us out. He *will* bring us out.

CHAPTER 6
Destiny

Do you know what your spiritual gift is? Do you know God's destiny and/or calling for your life? Romans 11:29 reads, "For the gifts and calling of God are without repentance." (KJV) As a child of God, you need to know and understand what your destiny is. If you desire to get married, you need to understand first that you are not just saved to be saved. You are not just born again to warm a pew in your local church. God did not redeem you simply to give you a free ride to Heaven.

Just like Jeremiah the prophet (Jeremiah 1:5), God knew you before you were formed in your mother's belly; He has a purpose and a plan for your life. You need to know what that plan is before you get married. You need to know that the man or woman you are courting is a part of God's plan for your life.

God showed me some 20 years ago that I was to preach the gospel. He also told me that I would be married to a preacher. I told Him, however, that I did not want that for my life. Because I understood the level of accountability that came with such a call and did not want to surrender, I began to run from God. It was as if I were running a marathon. Yes I had given my heart to God; I was born again. However, I had not *surrendered* my life and my will *completely* to Him. For many years I have had to suffer because of my decision. I was rejected by friends and family, I was physically, emotionally, verbally, and sexually abused, and I have suffered sickness and disease. I was spiritually oppressed, I was financially ruined, I lost my marriage, I lost my home and all of my possessions, I almost lost my child, and many times I thought that I would lose my mind. If it had not been for the grace and mercy of God I would have lost my life.

Mr. David L. Robertson (ARIOSE Music Group, Inc) penned a song that was sung by Mr. David Binion and recorded by The Straight Gate Mass Choir on their CD *Expectations: I'll Praise*. The song entitled [1]"Say Goodbye to Me" tells the story of my surrender:

"Lord I want to be a servant of the King and I want my life to be inspired by all you bring; but for this I must die and sometimes it's hard to understand the reasons why. Isn't there some way I can save a piece of me; isn't there somehow you can take this cup from me; but I hear you whispering this is how it has to be—but my God it's awfully hard to say goodbye to me. Hold me close as I say goodbye to me; let my heart know that you are all I need. I'll stay right here on my knees until I find the strength to say goodbye to me—cause I'm tired of living somewhere in between my love for you and my love for me. So take whatever's left of me, I sacrifice it Lord to thee... Goodbye, to me." The second verse says: "Help me cast down every idol that I've built, and lay them all where Calvary's blood was spilt; there where you sacrificed your life for me—now it's my turn Lord to die for thee".

What a powerful song; can any of you relate to this? Has the

---

1 Say Goodbye to Me – Written by: David L. Robertson ARIOSE MUSIC GROUP, INC., Lead Vocal: David Binion (CD: The Straight Gate Mass Choir "Expectations: I'll Praise" Bajada Records ©2003)

Lord called you to do something that you feel you are not qualified, or *ready* to do?

Matthew 16:24-25 says "Then said Jesus unto his disciples, If any man will come after me, let him deny himself, and take up his cross, and follow me. For whosoever will save his life shall lose it: and whosoever will lose his life for my sake shall find it." (KJV) You see, I did not want to *die*. I was trying to *save* my life. But I had to go to the cross and die. Jesus told the Apostle Paul "...it is hard for thee to kick against the pricks." (Acts 9:5b KJV) And remember, He was speaking [at that time] to Saul; this was prior to the conversion—prior to the 'yes Lord'! You see, I had been kicking and kicking, until I could not kick any more. I had been beat down by the devil long enough. I was tired of fighting—tired of running. I finally decided to surrender.

Numbers 23:19 reads "God is not a man, that he should lie; neither the son of man, that he should repent: hath he said, and shall he not do it? Or hath he spoken, and shall he not make it good?" (KJV) Ladies, God is not going to change His mind about what He has called you to be just because you are living the life of a *Gomer* (read Hosea chapters 1-3). Gentlemen, if God is calling you to go to Nineveh (read Jonah), then that is exactly where you will have to go.

I have found that when you tell God 'Yes', life is so much better. It will not always be a bed of roses, but there is a greater level of peace that comes with submission. The Bible says "Verily I say unto you, There is no man that hath left house, or brethren, or sisters, or father, or mother, or wife, or children, or lands, for my sake, and the gospel's, But he shall receive an hundredfold now in this time, houses, and brethren, and sisters, and mothers, and children, and lands, with persecutions; and in the world to come eternal life." (Mark 10:29-30 KJV) You see, surrender comes with a price. I can truly say, however, that it has been well worth the cost. 2 Timothy 2:11-12 says "It is a faithful saying: For if we be dead with him, we shall also live with him: If we suffer, we shall also reign with him: if we deny him, he also will deny us:" (KJV)

    Life is not worth living without Christ; He makes every day great! There was a time in my life when I did not even want to live. It took more energy than a little bit for me to get out of bed every day. But God has changed my heart and my life. He has done for me what no human being could have ever done. He has redeemed my soul, and renewed my mind. John 5:25 says, "Verily, verily, I say unto you, The hour is coming, and now is, when the dead shall hear the voice of the Son of God: and they that hear shall live." (KJV) I thank God for resurrecting me from the dead.

CHAPTER 7
Is it Real?

Did you know that when two believers marry, it is possible that they still be unequally yoked? It should not take rocket science to figure this out; however, I was at a very desperate time in my life. As I recall the days and nights I spent in prayer during my early years of marriage, God began to remind me of the dream that He had given me many years before. He began to remind me of the calling that He had placed on my life. He began to show me visions of [my husband and] myself in ministry together. But I was still not ready to surrender.

Although I knew that I wanted out of my marriage, I agreed to go to counseling. My ex-husband and I sought counsel for the many problems that we had encountered in our marriage; but my heart was not in it. I had already made up my mind that I did not want ministry and that I did not want this marriage. I began the process of filing for a divorce and my ex-husband decided not to contest.

One month after I received my divorce, the most important person in my life (my grandmother) passed away. Six months later, I was on the brink of a nervous breakdown. I was miserable! I had gone back to partying and getting high, and was back in an unhealthy relationship with someone from my past. I had begun to do a fast spiral downward. After two years my family suffered another loss which was more than I could bear at that time in my life; I found myself in the psychiatric ward of a local hospital having a complete nervous breakdown. I did not want to live anymore; my life had no meaning and no purpose. Because I chose to do what I wanted to do instead of what God wanted me to do, I was [like Jonah] in my own whale's belly.

The Bible reads in Hebrews 10:31-33, "It is a fearful thing to fall into the hands of the living God. But recall the former days when, after you were enlightened, you endured a hard struggle with sufferings, sometimes being publicly exposed to abuse and affliction, and sometimes being partners with those so treated." (RSV) I had made my bed hard (as the old folks used to say), and now I had to lie in it.

I woke up one day and decided "I shall not die, but live, and declare the works of the Lord." (Psalm 118:17 KJV) I made up my mind that I was going to surrender and do what God was calling me to do.

One thing we all need to realize is that God's Word does not say that we are supposed to be *happy* in marriage *all the time*; it does not say we are to have everything our way. Genesis 2:18 says "And the Lord God said, It is not good that the man should be alone; I will make him a help meet for him." (KJV) The word 'help meet' signifies *suitable help*. Women are supposed to be of assistance to their husbands. Wives should not expect their husbands to treat them like a queen if they do not treat their husbands like the kings that they are.

Women have to be able to offer the man of God something else besides what is in between their legs. If the man has a dream and/or a vision the women needs to be able to contribute to that vision, all for the up building of the kingdom of God. If she cannot connect to the vision of the man of God and *help* him bring it to pass, then she should leave him alone; do not damage him. If you are married and your husband does not have a vision then it is up to you to tap into him and help him to recognize what it is that God has for him. Remember ladies, the Bible says that the man needs your *help*. You may not think you can be happy, but I guarantee you–there is nothing that can compare to the *joy of the Lord*.

Ephesians 5:22-24 reads, "Wives, submit yourselves unto your own husbands, as unto the Lord. For the husband is the head of the wife, even as Christ is the head of the church: and he is the savior of the body. Therefore as the church is subject unto Christ, so let the wives be to their own husbands in every thing." (KJV) Verse 33 says women are to *reverence* their husbands. The Greek word *Phobeomai* signifies being terrified or being afraid. Now do you see in Ephesians 5:23 where it says "...the husband is the head of the wife, even as Christ is the head of the church:" and in verse 32 where Paul writes "This is a great mystery: but I speak concerning Christ and the church." Follow me if you will.

Psalm 34:11 reads, "Come, ye children, hearken unto me: I will teach you the fear of the Lord". The Hebrew word *Yirah* means fear, terror, reverence, and awe. If a person truly recognizes God as El Shaddai (all-powerful), it will be seen in his or her attitude and daily life, in the form of reverence. So you see ladies, we are to reverence our husbands as the lords (notice small 'L') of our lives. Read also Psalm 111:10, Proverbs, 9:10, Proverbs 10:27, Proverbs 14:27, and Hebrews 12:28.

"Likewise, ye wives, be in subjection to your own husbands;

that, if any obey not the word, they also may without the word be won by the conversation of the wives; while they behold your chaste conversation coupled with fear. Whose adorning let it not be that outward adorning of plaiting the hair, and of wearing of gold, or of putting on of apparel; but let it be the hidden man of the heart, in that which is not corruptible, even the ornament of a meek and quiet spirit, which is in the sight of God of great price. For after this manner in the old time holy women also trusted in God, adorned themselves, being in subjection unto their own husbands: Even as Sarah obeyed Abraham, calling him lord: whose daughters ye are, as long as ye do well, and are not afraid with any amazement. Likewise, ye husbands, dwell with them according to knowledge, giving honor unto the wife, as unto the weaker vessel, and as being heirs together of the grace of life; that your prayers be not hindered." I Peter 3:1-7 (KJV).

We as women must realize that there are blessings in submission, but we have to learn the principle. Submission does not just begin in marriage. We must learn as children to submit to our parents (Ephesians 6:1); we must also learn (saved or unsaved) to submit to leadership (Hebrews 13:17). This submission is not just in the church. Ephesians 6:5 tells us, "Servants, be obedient to them that are your masters according to the flesh, with fear and trembling, in singleness of your heart, as unto Christ;" (KJV) Colossians 3:22 says, "Servants, obey in all things your masters according to the flesh; not with eyeservice, as men pleasers; but in singleness of heart, fearing God:" (KJV) More importantly, as children of God, James 4:7(a) exhorts "Submit yourselves therefore to God." (KJV) If we can learn the principle of submission *before* marriage and the blessings that ensue, then submission in marriage will not be a problem.

When we think about submission, there is often the thought of whether happiness can be found in submission. Happiness is not synonymous with joy. Nehemiah 8:10(b) says that the joy of the Lord is your strength. Philippians 4:6-7 reads, "Have no anxiety about anything, but in everything by prayer and supplication with thanksgiving let your requests be made known to God. And the peace of God, which passes all understanding, will keep your hearts and your minds in Christ Jesus (RSV).

We can have joy even if we do not feel happy. Joy is one of the fruit of the Spirit (Galatians 6). When things in our marriages do not seem to be going well, when the bills are not paid, and our spouses are not doing what we think they should be doing, we should not fuss and cuss. We should not throw things, not stop communicating, and not hold back on what we know we owe them (read I Corinthians 7:3-5). We must continue to honor our husbands, reverence them, pray for them, and continue to do what we are called to do as wives. God will bless us for our consistency and in the end he will bless our marriages. Keep in mind, our fight is not against flesh and blood (Ephesians 6:12). We must know who our enemy is; our husbands are not our enemies!

Women, we must always keep destiny at the forefront of our minds, knowing that others are watching; and more importantly, God is watching. Not only is He watching, but He is keeping a record. Someone else will be blessed by seeing you stand;

someone else's marriage will be helped if you do not let go. Happiness is based on *happenstances*. The joy of Jesus is forever. Regardless of what may be going on around you hold on, your help is on the way.

CHAPTER 8

Called to Be

It takes a tender heart and an attentive ear to be able to hear and know just what God is calling you to be. Ladies, I speak to you because I am a lady. I have been through, and am still going through many of the same things that you are going through. My goal is to be able to help just *one* somebody. If *one* person is blessed by this book, then its' purpose will have been fulfilled.

I trust that as you plan your weddings, you read as many books as you can on the subject. Study the Word of God in depth. Listen to as many tapes and CD's about marriage as you can. Arm yourself; you can never know too much. Be like a sponge; absorb all that you can. I cannot repeat this enough: marriage is not a joke!

Additionally, my sisters, we must learn some basic principles before we decide to marry. Do you have a stable job? Do you have a bank account? Can you manage a checkbook? Are you credit worthy? Do you have mounds and mounds of debt? Do you own a home? What do you have to bring to the table? What help can you offer to the man of God? Remember, we are supposed to be suitable help. As I said before, you should be able to offer the man of God more than just sex. What is left after the orgasm? We need not be so absorbed with simply finding someone to take care of us.

The Proverbs 31 woman was self-sufficient; she was a businesswoman–an entrepreneur. She had it going on. She was not consumed with finding a man to take care of her. For those who may be unfamiliar with this [popular] proverb, let us visit it together.

Proverbs 31 is the last chapter in the book; it is known as an acrostic poem, similar to Psalm 119 in which all 22 letters of the Hebrew alphabet are used in sequence [to begin each verse]. A foot note in the [2]Hebrew-Greek Key Study Bible reads: "This poem sings the praises of a good wife. It extols the honor and dignity of women, and emphasizes the importance of the mother in the home. The secret of her dignity and honor is that she "fears the Lord" (v. 30). As a result, her husband trusts in her, and she becomes a source of honor to her whole family. The poem does not criticize physical beauty as some claim (v. 30); it merely asserts that being physically attractive is a temporary condition, while virtue has eternal worth." [Key 31: 10-31] KJV

Now let us read together these 22 verses entitled "A Good Woman":

Proverbs 31:10-31:

10 Who can find a virtuous woman? For her price is far above rubies. 11 The heart of her husband doth safely trust in her, so that he shall have no need of spoil. 12 She will do him good and not evil all the days of her life. 13 she seeketh wool, and flax, and worketh willingly with her hands. 14 She is like the merchants' ships; she bringeth her food from afar. 15 She riseth also while it is yet night, and giveth meat to her household and a portion to her maidens. 16 She considereth a field, and buyeth it: with the fruit of her hands she planteth a vineyard. 17 She girdeth her loins with strength, and

---

2 The Hebrew Greek Key Study Bible. (1991). Chattanooga, TN: AMG International, Inc. page 831

strengtheneth her arms. 18 She perceiveth that her merchandise is good: her candle goeth not out by night. 19 She layeth her hands to the spindle, and her hands hold the distaff. 20 She stretcheth out her hand to the poor; yea, she reacheth forth her hands to the needy. 21 She is not afraid of the snow for her household: for all her household are clothed with scarlet. 22 She maketh herself coverings of tapestry; her clothing is silk and purple. 23 Her husband is known in the gates, when he sitteth among the elders of the land. 24 She maketh fine linen, and selleth it; and delivereth girdles unto the merchant. 25 Strength and honor are her clothing, and she shall rejoice in time to come. 26 She openeth her mouth with wisdom, and in her tongue is the law of kindness. 27 She looketh well to the ways of her household, and eateth not the bread of idleness. 28 Her children arise up, and call her blessed; her husband also, and he praiseth her. 29 Many daughters have done virtuously, but thou excellest them all. 30 Favor is deceitful and beauty is vain: but a woman that feareth the Lord, she shall be praised. 31 Give her of the fruit of her hands; and let her own works praise her in the gates."

    WOW! That is a mouth full. Now let us delve into a few of these verses a little deeper. Verse 11 says, "The heart of her husband doth safely trust in her". This woman did not seek to marry a man simply to have help paying her bills. She did not marry with the assumption that she was going to be taken care of. She was of help to her husband; he could trust that she would not walk out on him when times got hard. No doubt, this woman would have been able to carry the family for a season if necessary. Verse 16 says, "...she considereth a field and buyeth it". It does not say that she required her husband's assistance in purchasing this field; she bought it with her own money. Which brings to mind another point: Have you checked your credit scores lately my sisters? (Please do not be offended, I'm ministering to myself as well—this is cutting me as deep as it is cutting some of you). This sister worked hard and earned her own living; she was a help meet to her husband. She was B-A-D! This woman was a power-house. She did not waste her husband's money, nor did she waste her own. She knew how to B-U-D-G-E-T! (Ouch!!!)

This woman that the 31st chapter of Proverbs is speaking of, no doubt, was a bargain shopper. She probably did not shop at Niemann Marcus™, Lord and Taylor™, or any of the other high-end department stores that we are familiar with. She could sew. She made clothes for her family, saving her husband loads of money. No doubt, she had a savings account.

Ladies, let us educate ourselves before we go out searching for a husband; actually, we should not even be out searching. But let us be educated on a few things: First, financial seminars are not taboo. If we know that we have issues handling money, it is okay for us to seek advice and/or direction from those who are expert in that subject. It is also okay, ladies, to shop at thrift stores [oh, no she did not go there]... oh yes I did!

Child of God, John the Apostle wrote in his third epistle "Beloved, I wish above all things that thou mayest prosper and be in health, even as thy soul prospereth" (I John 3:2 KJV). The word of God is loaded with financial principles. Ladies, let us find ourselves independently prosperous so as not to be a burden to the man of God when the Lord sends him.

And when you do finally meet someone, do not be in such a hurry that you miss God. Do not just look for someone who is saved. Do not just look at the physique. You know how you like them: 6 feet tall, black as berry juice, and bald, or light skinned with fine curly hair, and green or hazel eyes. You know what I mean. Think again; does he love the Lord? Is he committed to a local church? Is he submitted to authority? Can he receive instruction? Do not allow a man to require you to submit if he has not, himself, learned to do so. If you read Ephesians the 5th chapter and the 21st verse, both men and women are instructed to submit themselves one to another "in the fear of the Lord".

It may take some time, ladies, to find out all you need to know about a man before you marry; additionally gentlemen, it will take some time for you to find out all you need to know about that cutie pie you want to take home to meet your mother. I learned in counseling many years ago that couples should date for a minimum of one year; this affords the opportunity to experience each other throughout each season. How many of you [ladies and gentlemen] can be honest and acknowledge that some of us could be mistaken for 'chameleons'? You know that lizard-like creature that changes colors? Dictionary.com defines a chameleon as a person who is changeable, fickle, or inconsistent. Does that sound familiar to anyone? Let us consider this past year; think back to your winter, spring, summer, and fall. This may not be pleasant, but it could be life saving.

Ladies and gentleman, we must also assure that an individual is holding down a steady job; we do not need inconsistency in work records... hopping from one job to the next every several months. Ladies, if the gentleman has children from a previous [marriage] relationship, do you see him taking care of his children? Is he in court for past due child support? These are questions that need to be answered.

If the two of you are busy in ministry and both are focused on God, then He will reveal to [not one], both of you His plan for your lives.

Do not be charmed ladies by his 'suave-ness'; gentlemen, do not allow the softness and the sweetness of her voice keep you from hearing God. And finally, I beg you both; *PLEASE...* do not entertain the thought of sex. Experience has taught us all too well that when things do not work out, the pain and devastation only leads to depression, oppression, backsliding, soul ties, and even spiritual death. Ladies and gentlemen, one moment of pleasure is not worth losing your anointing, your place in God, and more importantly, your position in eternity.

I once received a prophecy that everything I needed (comfort, companionship, healing, deliverance, etc.) would come through worship. I had a conversation with a co-worker some time ago (who also happened to be a minister), who shared that God wants to get us to a place where we know that *He* is all that we need. When we get to that place in worship (men and women alike), God will then know that it is safe for Him to send us a mate because it is then and only then that He can trust that we will not put that person before

Him. The first commandment (Exodus 20:3) is that we are to have no other gods before Him. When God knows that He can trust us not to cheat on Him, then our Romeo's and Juliet's will be sent.

CHAPTER 9
Basic Training

Do you know anyone who has served in the Armed Forces? I was speaking with my younger brother, who served in the United States Army; we were talking about basic training (boot camp). I liken the training that we are receiving in God's spiritual army to that of the military training received in the Armed Forces. My brother shared with me that boot camp involves intense training and strengthening.

Before you leave home to travel abroad, you may need to receive vaccinations and/or immunizations due to the different strains of disease in other parts of the world. Likewise, if you are not immunized [in the spirit], you may have to go through different tests and trials to get you ready to go to other parts of the world (as commanded in Matthew 28:19). You have to read your Bible, pray, and fast in order to immunize yourself and protect against different strains of [spiritual] disease. Boot camp is usually about eight weeks, after which some recruits will go through an additional six weeks of advanced infantry training (depending on the specialty they chose). In God's army, the spiritual army, we are not given the option of choosing a specialty. God knew before the foundations of the world what we were destined to be in Him (read Jeremiah 1:5). Each of us must go through our own individual advanced infantry training [in the spirit] based on the calling that God has on our lives. Someone who is going to have a worldwide ministry, a demon fighting, devil chasing anointing, will have to go through more intense preparation and/or training (meaning more trials and tribulations) than the average Christian. If you are comfortable in your local church sitting and warming a pew, or if you sing on the choir, or usher on the usher board, it may not be necessary for you to endure [advanced infantry training].

If you ever get serious and decide you are concerned about souls–start evangelizing and witnessing to the lost (speaking boldly to people about their sin), then God will know that He can really trust you. When you begin to pray for your Pastor instead of talking about him then heaven will begin to move on your behalf. When you begin to acknowledge what it is that God has called you to do, and you get serious about doing it, then your battle with the enemy will really begin.

My brother shared with me that it is not unusual for soldiers in the military to be awakened with loud horns, with yelling, and with banging on trash cans and doors at 4:00a.m. Likewise, in the spiritual army, you may be awakened [by the Holy Spirit] at any hour that may not be comfortable and/or convenient [for you]. You may be called to go and minister to someone; someone whom you may not be very fond of. The master sergeant in the military can make you stop, drop, and do push-ups or any other physical task at any time for no reason at all. There may be other forms of punishment [discipline] that superiors may use to break individuals down in order to rebuild them to their standards.

During sensitivity training or survival training, soldiers are taught to shoot their weapons; they learn how to navigate through the wilderness and how to preserve their physical bodies. They are also taught how to deal with adverse circumstances. After a soldier goes through basic military training he/she becomes a different person; better...stronger. I also spoke with a navy seaman who shared with me that basic military training does not just prepare an individual physically, but mentally as well. He explained that recruits must learn to navigate and always be aware of their surroundings. "We had to learn to improvise..." he said.

Additionally, I learned that MRE's (meals ready to eat) are rations that soldiers received while out in the fields. These rations were worse than [frozen] TV dinners. There were times when soldiers were not able to eat. Depending on the length of an assignment, it sometimes became necessary to stretch what was provided. Soldiers had to condition themselves to be able to endure at times without eating a thing. Likewise, in the spiritual army, we may have to sacrifice meals (fast and pray) in order to condition ourselves to endure tests and trials as they come.

The Bible tells us that Daniel proclaimed a fast (read the 1st chapter of the book of Daniel). "...at the end of ten days their countenances appeared fairer and fatter in flesh than all the children which did eat the portion of the king's meat (Daniel 1:15 KJV).

Boot camp is a test of your will; everyone who starts out may not finish; the same goes for marriage. The scripture encourages us, however, in Ecclesiastes the 9th chapter and the 11th verse "...that the race is not to the swift, nor the battle to the strong" (KJV) Boot Camp is designed to change your way of thinking, to condition your body, to change your will, and to break you emotionally. The point is, just as we are instructed in 2nd Timothy 2:3 ("Thou therefore endure hardness, as a good soldier of Jesus Christ.") we need to be changed in the spirit of our minds (read Romans 12:1-2) in order that Christ may use us as He sees fit, and give us what [who] He thinks we should have in our lives. (Read also Philippians 4:7-8, I Timothy 6:12, Ephesians 4:11-12, I Peter 4:12-13, I Peter 4:1, and Ephesians 6:10-18 for encouragement.)

Child of God, do not get tired of standing; do not get tired of waiting on the Lord to send you His best. As you wait on the Lord (Psalm 27:14, Isaiah 40:31) to prepare that perfect someone for you, the Lord is also preparing you for that special someone. Remember, our trials are not in vain; they have a purpose.

Romans 5:3-5 reads: "And not only so, but we glory in tribulations also: knowing that tribulation worketh patience; and patience, experience; and experience, hope: And hope maketh not ashamed; because the love of God is shed abroad in our hearts by the Holy Ghost which is given unto us." The old folks used to sing a song years ago "...put your time in, pay day is coming after a while..." Put your time in young people; your pay day is coming after a while.

CHAPTER 10

He Loves Me, He Loves Me Not

I am reminded of the fairy tale Cinderella. Cinderella must have been damaged emotionally because she grew up in a home with a wicked stepmother, two wicked step sisters, and no father. The story did not tell us that she had any other family, no aunts, uncles, or cousins. She had no friends, no one to visit her, and no one for her to visit. Cinderella, it appeared, was trapped.

No doubt, Cinderella was very lonely. She was forced to do all of the housework. I am sure that she must have felt unappreciated on many occasions, and she probably felt that she was good for nothing. Cinderella did not go out shopping with the girls; she did not hang out at the mall. She did not go to movies; she did not go to school dances. Comparatively speaking, the ball was probably like going to a high school prom. Cinderella was not invited–and not expected to be there. Her stepmother and her stepsisters probably did not think that she was good enough, smart enough, or pretty enough. But who are *they*?

Validation is another reason why some choose to marry; they may feel that they need to have someone in their life in order to make them feel valuable and/or important. Do you realize that you do not need people to validate you? What does God's word say about you? Cinderella did not have anyone to tell her that she was loved. She did not have anyone to tell her that she was special, that she mattered, that she was pretty, or that she was smart. Her stepmother and stepsisters never told her that they were proud of her. Cinderella probably longed for the day that she would grow up and be able to leave that house and be away from those wicked people, never to look back.

Her dreams began to come true when her fairy godmother showed up and made a way for her to go to the ball. She wore a beautiful gown, rode in a horse-driven carriage, and experienced an evening of heaven on earth, dancing with a handsome prince. It all came to a screeching halt, however, at midnight.

Have you ever had a midnight experience? Have you ever had a time in your life where it seemed that everything you ever loved was lost? Do you sometimes feel that everything in life that causes you happiness somehow fades away into nothingness?

Unfortunately for many of us, life does not end with 'happily ever after' as Cinderella's life did. Many people get married in an attempt to escape the memories of a painful past. Some think that when they get married they will be able to somehow erase and/or forget all of the pain and emptiness of a miserable past. Regrettably, all of the pain, misery, and baggage of our pasts will follow us into our future. Unless past hurts are healed, issues will follow us into adulthood and into our marriages.

We see others getting married and think that their lives are just simply wonderful. Big extravagant weddings—long romantic honey moons can be a façade. Do not let the enemy trick you into believing that the grass is greener on the other side of the fence; as the saying goes, 'everything that glitters ain't gold'. Now I know that this is not grammatically correct, but unfortunately, for many people the grass on the other side is artificial turf and the glitter is just gold plated. We may never know *all* of the hell that some married couples endure.

The enemy will not show you 'hell' in someone else's marriage. He will only magnify how lonely you are and how many bills you have to pay (by yourself). He will put emphasis on how you are raising those hard-headed children by yourself and how stressed out you are. The enemy will not tell you that the girl next door has to deal with verbal and emotional abuse from her husband. He will not tell you that your girlfriend's husband is spending his pay check at the strip joint and/or gambling, and that she is *still* paying all of the bills by herself. You may never know that Sister Susie's husband was abused as a child and that he witnessed his mother being abused by his father. Sister Susie did not even know that; she did not know her husband for a full year before they wed. Now Sister Susie is covering up black eyes with make-up and dark sun glasses, and missing the PTA meetings at school; the afternoon socials at the country club are unimportant and go unattended. Sister Susie will not tell you the truth, however; she will continue to make excuses [one after another] and cover up for this man whom she thought that she loved. She will not tell you the truth because she wants you [and everyone else] to believe that her life is wonderful. After all, she was in such a rush to get married; she just knew that she had heard from God. Now Sister Susie has to admit that, yes, she missed God!

Ladies, how many of you can be honest and say that you can relate to this situation: A woman loves a man before she is born again; they are in a very heated relationship. Everything *seems* wonderful. He loves her as much as she loves him. This woman has an experience in a church service one night and accepts Jesus Christ as her Lord and Savior. She comes home and tells this man that she has accepted Christ and now she is saved; she begins to explain to him that things will have to change. It is hard at first but, eventually, he agrees to move out.

The couple continues to see each other even after he has moved out; long telephone conversations, occasional dates, and yes, even good night kisses. He is trying to understand her new life and her personal convictions. He has agreed not to force her into having sex (unless of course *she* wants to). He begins to tell her that they are going to get married *one day*. This woman continues in church, continues in her relationship, and continues to believe that this man loves her. She has no reason to doubt him when he promises her that they will soon be married. Five years turns into ten years; ten years turns into fifteen years; still no ring.

Finally, after twenty years has passed, the young lady begins to reason within herself that this man has no intention of marrying her; she decides to move on with her life. After twenty years, however, she finds herself frustrated and broken. She does not know where to begin in this endeavor to *'move on'*. She has never loved anyone else in her life; she has told the Lord that if she cannot have this man she would rather be by herself. Tell me ladies, where do we find the beginning of 'begin again'?

It is so very sad that this woman, and many others like her, cannot believe that God could have a plan for their lives (read Jeremiah 29:11). There is a man of God tailor-made for you (and for me), but many of us have closed our hearts and minds to the possibility of him ever finding us. Notice I said *"him ever finding us"*. What happened to this woman in her younger years that has caused her to believe that she did not deserve any better? What happened to you?

Kimberly Davis notes "The truth is that many African-American women are on a heart search for their soul mate or a soul search for their heart mate and are coming up empty."[3] The writer of the article notes that "many of them are frustrated in their search, some would say even desperate, for a husband." Women are drawn to magazine articles such as the one found in [February 2007] ESSENCE™ with catchy headings on the cover "28-DAY DATING PLAN: Where to Meet Him, What to Say, How to Make Him Yours"[4]; or the one noted on the cover of the [October 2007] issue of ESSENCE™ entitled "30 Dates in 30 Days". In this particular segment the public is introduced to five single women, and solicited over a period of 30 days to go on-line and help these women find love[5]. The magazine tells us that over 400 ladies responded to the call.

Reality television shows giving women the opportunity to date countless men and pick one from the bunch, as if this is destiny.

---

3 Davis, Kimberly. SOS for Single Christian Sisters. Ebony Volume LX, Number 3. 2005, January pp104

4 Jumaralli, Zulaika, 30 Dates in 30 Days. Essence Volume 38, Number 6. 2007, October pp 193

5 Malkin, Nina. Essence Truth or Dare Dating Challenge. Essence Volume 27, Number 10. 2007, February pp179

Speed-dating and on-line dating are proof that we are a society living in desperate times. One woman had such a profound experience, that she decided it was worth putting on paper. She penned a book entitled: "Better Single than Sorry"[6]. This woman decided that she wanted to let the world know that desperation is not ladylike and that women can be satisfied single.

Ladies, we do not need to receive flowers from a man to determine if that man really loves us. We must stop picking off the rose petals [in our minds] and saying to ourselves: "he loves me, he loves me not". Take a serious look at the entire picture. Am I an integral part of this man's life? Have I been home to meet his family? Do we go out [in public] on dates or is it always just personal visits to *my* home? Why has he not invited me to *his* home? Do we spend holidays together? Do we fellowship together in church? Does he even attend church? What do we have in common? Are we both speaking of a future, or am I doing all of the talking? Finally, does he try to pressure me into having sex even after I have expressed a desire to remain celibate?

Sweetheart, face it, this man does not love you, and he has no intention of marrying you. It is time for you to move on; get in God's face. Begin to let God heal you-let Him begin to show you what [real] love is. I guarantee that as soon as you begin to let God in [completely] He will send a man who will not only love you, but who will love you as Christ commands in Ephesians 5:25, 28-29. Matthew 6:33 tells us to seek God's kingdom first, and everything

---

6 Schefft, Jen. Better Single than Sorry. Harper Collins. New York, NY: 2007

else in life that we desire will be given.

As you pluck the petals off the rose, wondering within yourself if he really loves you, God's answer will always be: "yes, I really love you".

CHAPTER 11
Alone, But Not Lonely

I can remember more than 15 years ago being in a prayer line and having a prophet tell me that just because I was alone did not mean that I had to be lonely. He told me that God had a special love for me that was just for me. I recall this man of God telling me that the love that God had was such that it could be compared to no physical love I had ever or would ever experience.

Some time after that as I was reading the Word of God I came across Ephesians 3:16-20; I nearly leaped out of my skin. I called my sister [in Christ] on the telephone. Up to that point in my walk with the Lord, I had not ever read (or do not recall reading) that scripture. I told my sister that God put this scripture in the Bible just for me. It meant so much to me to know that God *really* loved me, and that he wanted me to be happy.

After all the many years I had searched, all the men, all the nights I cried and begged them to love me, God Himself was already loving me.

When we are born, we are born with a purpose. When we are born *again*, we are also born *again* with a purpose. When we get married, we have a purpose. God has a specific purpose for everything in our lives-from the moment we are conceived. When I began to realize my *true* purpose for existing, I finally realized what God meant when He told me, 'It is not about you'. Isaiah 43:6(b)-7 says "Bring my sons from afar and my daughters from the ends of the earth-everyone who is called by my name, whom I created for my glory, whom I formed and made." (Today's NIV) I realized that the Lord had created me [and you] for the sole purpose of bringing glory to God.

Revelation 4:11 says "Thou art worthy, O Lord to receive glory and honour and power: for thou hast created all things, and for thy pleasure they are and were created." (KJV) God created us for His pleasure. Because we have been created for God's pleasure, we are commanded in I Corinthians 10:31 "So whether you eat or drink or whatever you do, do it all for the glory of God." (Today's NIV)

I have spent many years frustrated because I did not have anyone to come home to every evening. I did not have anyone to do man-work around the house. I did not have anyone to work on my vehicle when it needed repair. I recall that it was even frustrating for me to be sick, because I did not have anyone to take me to the doctor or care for me when I got home. I craved attention; I wanted someone to nurse me back to health as I had done for so many others when they were sick. Many may believe that the brothers and sisters in the church can serve these purposes for the single [saints] however, we need to be honest with ourselves [and with God]; we need to admit that we get tired of our brothers and sisters in Christ serving as a crutch for what [who] we are really seeking in our lives—a true companion. I did not believe that the church could fill *every* void in my life during my single years, and many of you don't believe that now. No matter how much we stayed in church we still experienced loneliness. We have attended many singles ministry meetings; we have gone to movies as a group and we have had countless bowling parties. We have had skating parties, panel discussions, and singles conferences that shook the walls of the church. We have full body pillows on our beds, and several stuffed teddy bears. Despite all this, however, lonely is still A-L-O-N-E!

There is, however, some good news for those like me who think the loneliness will never end. During those long nights amidst the tears, there is a song from heaven that can heal the brokenness and fill the emptiness. If you will allow, I can assure you that deliverance will come.

The ministry of music is a very powerful ministry. Music has been known to *sooth the savage beast*, when that beast in your life is loneliness, depression, discouragement, brokenness, or even thoughts of suicide, I encourage you to begin to worship.

When I spoke earlier about the perfect and complete love that I had discovered God had for me, I also realized something else; the presence of God is *real*. It can be [felt] as if someone was right there holding you tight in their arms. When we meditate on the word of God in prayer with music playing [in the background] strongholds can be broken, burdens can be removed, and yokes can be destroyed.

When I hear the old hymn 'Blessed Assurance' it quickens something in my spirit. When I listen to my favorite hymn of the church 'Tis So Sweet to Trust in Jesus' it awakens my faith. When I hear The Kurt Carr Singers proclaim "God Blocked It"[7] I am reminded of the miraculous work that God has wrought in my own

---

[7] "God Blocked It" CD: Kurt Carr Project "One Church" Zomba Gospel, LLC ©2005

life. When I hear Bishop Andrew Merritt and the Straight Gate Mass Choir sing their song "He Loves Me"[8] it reminds me that I never have to beg a man to love me and that I no longer need to search [endlessly] for that superficial emotion that neither satisfies nor lasts. When I hear Shekinah Glory Ministries sing their song "How Deeply I Need You"[9], I want to lay prostrate before the Lord and cry out to Him; invoking a presence that only worship can bring.

I believe that any [true] worshipper would agree—music is an art form that commands the very nature of a human being to be at peace in *any* situation. Let me also say, however, that even without music it is possible to experience God in a way that cannot be compared with any human experience, no matter how good that experience may have been.

Recorded in the book of the Prophet Ezekiel in the 28th chapter and the 11th through the 19th verses is this account of the heavenly choir master: "Moreover the word of the Lord came unto me, saying, Son of man, take up a lamentation upon the king of Tyrus, and say unto him, Thus saith the Lord God; Thou sealest up the sum, full of wisdom, and perfect in beauty Thou hast been in Eden the garden of God; every precious stone was thy covering, the sardius, topaz, and the diamond, the beryl, the onyx, and the jasper, the sapphire, the emerald, and the carbuncle, and gold: the workmanship of thy tabrets and of thy pipes was prepared in thee in

---

[8] "He Loves Me" (David Binion Music ASCAP) CD: The Straight Gate Mass Choir "Expectations: I'll Praise" Bajada Records ©2003

[9] "How Deeply I Need You" CD: Shekinah Glory Ministry "Live" Kingdom Records Music ©2004

the day that thou wast created. Thou are the anointed cherub that covereth; and I have set thee so: thou wast upon the holy mountain of God; thou hast walked up and down in the midst of the stones of fire. Thou wast perfect in thy ways from the day that thou wast created, till iniquity was found in thee. By the multitude of thy merchandise they have filled the midst of thee with violence, and thou hast sinned: therefore I will cast thee as profane out of the mountain of God: and I will destroy thee. O covering cherub, from the midst of the stones of fire. Thine heart was lifted up because of thy beauty; thou hast corrupted thy wisdom by reason of thy brightness: I will cast thee to the ground. I will lay thee before kings, that they may behold thee. Thou hast defiled thy sanctuaries by the multitude of thine iniquities, by the iniquity of thy traffic; therefore will I bring forth a fire from the midst of thee, it shall devour thee, and I will bring thee to ashes upon the earth in the sight of all them that behold thee. All they that know thee among the people shall be astonished at thee: thou shalt be a terror, and never shalt thou be any more." (KJV) WOW!

How many of you knew that satan himself, the heavenly choir-master, arrayed in beauty, majesty, and splendor, was [from the beginning of time] anointed to bring deliverance to mankind through music? The music came directly from him. He walked and music played. Each step a tune—a melody. Because of lucifer's pride, however, Isaiah 14:12-14 lets us know that he was kicked out of heaven; dethroned so to speak.

From the beginning of time, before God ever gave Adam his Eve, He provided for Adam in the Garden of Eden everything necessary for a worship experience. Genesis chapter 2 and verse 8 tells us that God planted a garden and placed the man therein. In that garden was everything that God created (according to the creation account in Genesis chapter 1). Verses 9 through 14 describe such beauty and splendor; a most heavenly place no doubt suitable for unimaginable worship experiences.

There was the man (Adam), there was the majesty of the heavenly choir-master (lucifer), and there was God himself. Genesis 3:8 lets us know that Adam could indeed experience intimate fellowship with God [in the flesh]. Adam experienced "theophanies," which Webster's defines as manifestations (or appearances) of God to a person. Much like an epiphany, but Adam had these experiences repeatedly.

No doubt, when Eve came on the scene, she took up time with Adam that satan [then called lucifer] probably wanted. I am sure that Eve distracted Adam so that satan no longer had his attention. God, however, understood the purpose of the woman; after all, He was the one who saw the need of the man. That is why He [God] created the woman; God knew that it was "...not good that the man should be alone..." (Genesis 2:18).

It was *supposed to be* from the beginning of time that man would live forever in the garden and experience God continually. And so when the woman was created, she was created to fulfill a need that the man had [that lucifer could not fulfill].

Adam and Eve were instructed to be fruitful, to multiply, and to replenish the earth (Genesis 1:28). The woman was not supposed to, however, take away from Adam's private worship experiences and his times of intimate fellowship with God.

In the same way, our mates should not take us away from what is supposed to be [ordained from the beginning of time to be] personal, intimate, communion and fellowship with God our maker. We all need that time to love on God and let Him love on us; to let Him know how much we appreciate Him. We must never cease to let God know how much we need Him, and to let Him know how strong our desires are toward Him. He needs to know how much our very lives depend on Him. This should be something we all experience before marriage, and continue to experience (even the more) after marriage.

CHAPTER 12

Still Not Delivered

Awakened one night from a sound sleep, I was challenged in my spirit as I heard (the enemy) questioning: "What qualifies you to write this book? You are still not delivered, yourself." I was dumb founded. As I lay quietly in my bed with tears streaming down my face all I could think was: the book is nearly completed. I could see in my mind a published work within a six-month view. I thought of the scripture in Luke 17:14(b) which says "...And it came to pass, that, as they went, they were cleansed."

The Greek word *katharizo* which is derived from *katharos* means: to cleanse or to free from filth. It signifies being cleansed in the sense of purification (from a spiritual stand-point). It also signifies being purified from pollution and the guilt of sin. Webster's defines catharsis as the purging of the emotions or relieving of emotional tension especially through a work of art (as of tragedy or music); a discharge of repressed or pent-up emotions resulting in the alleviation of symptoms or the elimination of the condition.

Katharos is the root word from which we derive our (English) word – cathartic or cathartical, which is defined as an evacuating or purging of the bowels. My friends, there is nothing like a good laxative (if you will allow me to compare) to clean us out when we are all backed up. There may come a time when God finds it necessary to 'clean us out' [in the Spirit], and rid us of all the unnecessary junk that we may be holding on to. David asked the

Lord in the 51st division of the Psalms in verse 7: "Purge me with hyssop, and I shall be clean". How many of us truly want the Lord to purge us?

As I began to reminisce about a conference I attended in Englewood, Ohio back in July 2006 the Lord reminded me of the prophecy that was spoken. I had just completed my first book, "EL SHADDAI: God My Sufficiency" (Rivers of Living Water Publishing © 2007), and had begun to work on this project. The prophecy was concerning the completion of this project. It was spoken that I still had unresolved hurts and emotions within that had not yet been healed; areas in my life that I had not allowed the Holy Spirit to touch. I was told that as I wrote, different cells would be opened and healing would take place. I began to imagine in my mind a cell block inside of a prison. Emotions that had been suppressed for years began to be released and healed as I wrote. I could hear (in the spirit) chains falling off; I could see prison doors opening and I could (feel and) see myself being set free in many areas in my life.

When people are released from prison, they are not all released at the same time; neither are they all released to the same place. Some are released to halfway houses and some to their own homes with their families. Some may find it difficult to remain free due to the challenge of having to reacclimate to society. For those who had been incarcerated for extended periods of time, a normal life 'on the streets' will not only be foreign, but may be unobtainable. What is *normal*? Having to adjust to freedom, having to obtain employment, having to pay bills, having to change old habits and patterns of thought, are just a few of the ways in which ex-cons will have to adjust in order to obtain normalcy and remain free. For those who are able to adapt and remain free, it matters not where they have been released to; all that matters is that they are free.

I do not wish to concern myself with where all the old hurts, emotions, and baggage from my past has gone; neither will I focus on when they were released [healed]. All I know is that I have been set free by the power of God and am no longer in bondage.

Please do not allow the enemy to discourage you, keeping you bound in your mind concerning deliverance. You cannot stay bound; true deliverance will manifest itself, and you will know when it does. We must understand, however, that [the state of] being delivered is not a destination-it is a journey. We must continue in prayer, we have to fast on occasion; we must constantly crucify our flesh. The moment we begin to think that we have *reached* that destination (deliverance) and say within ourselves "I've finally arrived", a fine specimen of a man [or woman] wrapped in snake skin will slither past. Before we know it we will be caught up – AGAIN!!! It is at that moment that we must open our spiritual ears and hear the Holy Spirit as he begins to sweetly whisper "...you are not ready; get back on your knees...". We must know down in our "spiritual knower" when we are being called to marriage. Not only when, but to whom we are being called to marry, and at what season. Remember, God does EVERYTHING descent and in order.

If you will recall the woman with the issue of blood in Luke 8:43-48; she did not care who was in the crowd. She did not concern herself with who knew her past. When we need something from the

Lord we cannot let these things concern us. This woman, whose name we do not know, did not stop to think that someone else was speaking to Jesus; she ignored all protocol, forgot her manners, and began to 'press' her way through the crowd. She pressed, as we are instructed to do in Philippians chapter 3 and verses 12-15: "Not as though I had already attained, either were already perfect: but I follow after, if that I may apprehend that for which also I am apprehended of Christ Jesus. Brethren, I count not my self to have apprehended: but this one thing I do, forgetting those things which are behind, and reaching forth unto those things which are before, I press toward the mark for the prize of the high calling of God in Christ Jesus. Let us therefore, as many as be perfect, be thus minded: and if in any thing ye be otherwise minded, God shall reveal even this unto you." (KJV)

Holiness is not popular, but it is still right; and it requires a true 'press' through all of life's hard circumstances and situations that may come our way.

CHAPTER 13

Don't Be Discouraged

As I sat in a youth service many years ago, I began to be discouraged by the testimonies of others. Some spoke about how the Lord had been keeping them, about the things that God had spoken to them, and about where they were in their Christian walk. I began to think about how long I had been saved; I thought about all the years I did not trust God and continued in my own way. I began to reminisce about all the many times I had fallen and how [afterwards] I realized that it really was not worth it. I began to think about the relationships I had been in, and how they kept me from what God had for me. I could blame no one but myself.

Do not be discouraged by the testimony of others, and do not allow yourself to get distracted by time (read II Peter 3:8). Yes, God understands that it has been a long time, and that you have been waiting patiently for Him to send you a mate. But there may be some areas in our lives where God still has to 'grow us up'; we must remember that God knows better than we do.

We used to sing a hymn years ago "...each victory will help you some other to win..." Romans 3:23 says, "For all have sinned, and come short of the glory of God;" (KJV). Each situation that we have had to endure in life was necessary for us to learn to appreciate God. Think about it...where would you be if you had not learned to trust God through all that you have experienced in life? Thank God for your experiences-don't down-play them; they made you who you are today. Now I am in no way trying to make light of sin, however, there are some who call themselves Christians, who will attempt to belittle you or try to make you feel less saved (if there is such a term) because you are not living a *perfect* life [as if they are]. Kindly let them know "God knew I needed that experience in my life because my experience will help someone else one day." Don't let the 'super-saints' hold you back. Because some people do not smoke, drink, cuss, gamble, lie, cheat, steal, and lay up anymore, they may try to tell you that you are not saved (if you still struggle in any of these areas). My Bible tells me "That if thou shalt confess with thy mouth the Lord Jesus, and shalt believe in thine heart that God hath raised him from the dead, thou shalt be saved. For with the heart man believeth unto righteousness; and with the mouth confession is made unto salvation." (Romans 10:9-10 KJV)

Paul and Silas told the keeper of the prison [who asked the question in Acts 16:30 "...Sirs, what must I do to be saved?"] exactly what was required of him in order to obtain salvation. "And they said, Believe on the Lord Jesus Christ, and thou shalt be saved, and thy house." (Acts 16:31 KJV) The requirements for salvation are simply to confess, believe, and receive. The Bible declares that you *will* be saved. Child of God do not allow anyone to try to tell you that you are not saved.

Now after salvation, comes a closer walk with the Lord; (God and) time will produce in you a greater desire for holiness and sanctification. You will begin to lose your desire for any habit that is not pleasing to God. But you must get your eyes off people because people will hinder you. Peter began to sink [read Matthew 14:28-31] when he took his eyes off Jesus. Keep your eyes on the Lord-He is the only one who can save you and keep you.

In the book of Hebrews the 12th chapter verses 1-2(a), we are exhorted: "Wherefore seeing we also are compassed about with so great a cloud of witnesses, let us lay aside every weight, and the sin which doth so easily beset us, and let us run with patience the race that is set before us, Looking unto Jesus the author and finisher of our faith;..." (KJV) The Holy Spirit will begin to convict you every time you do something that displeases Him. One day you will wake up and realize that you have not only abstained from sin, but that you do not even have a desire to sin any more. Your main focus will be on pleasing God. No matter what is going on, be encouraged.

CHAPTER 14

Walk the Walk

Paul in Ephesians 4:1-3 writes "I therefore, the prisoner of the Lord, beseech you that ye walk worthy of the vocation wherewith ye are called, with all lowliness and meekness, with longsuffering, forbearing one another in love; Endeavoring to keep the unity of the Spirit in the bond of peace." (KJV)

Let us now look at how to 'walk the walk' of a child of God. I like to look at it from the stand point of a job; those of us who have been saved for any period of time understand that it takes 'work' to live *right*.

Now for those of you 'holier than thou' Christians who think that salvation is just another walk in the park, this is not for you. For those of you who are skating through this Christian walk on your 'flowery bed of ease' and are having no trouble living right, I am not speaking to you right now. I want to talk to those true soldiers who put on their armor every day before they leave home; those 'for real' saints [those of us] who work a nine to five everyday surrounded by unsaved folks who get on your nerves and [almost] get cussed out. Let me have your attention for a while, if I may.

The word 'vocation' in the Greek *klésis* is translated *a calling; a condition; employment.* When we get saved, we realize that it takes some work for us to change our ways; we cannot do the same things that we used to do and call ourselves Christians. We need to be changed in our minds, our wills, and our emotions. The world needs to see this change in us in order to know that we are truly who we profess to be.

When we think about getting married, we must realize that marriage, like being a Christian, will be work. Marriage is a vocation. Some refer to it as a 'calling' or a ministry. Just like singing in the choir, serving on the usher board, and/or teaching in the Sunday school, marriage will require [years of] preparation and practice. There is a need for weekly (or sometimes daily) meetings, and there are dues (obligations) that must be paid. This vocation requires commitment and sacrifice—this is a job for 'grown folks'.

We are instructed in Ephesians 4:2 "With all lowliness and meekness, with longsuffering..." to forebear others; that means we must put up with some stuff from individuals that may not be pleasant. The word longsuffering is taken from the Greek *makrothumia* (or *makrothumeo*) which also translates 'patience'.

The Bible also says that "...tribulation worketh patience;" (Romans 5:3b). So it will only be that the 'going through' in life and in marriage will teach us how to endure. Longsuffering is not something that we will get in our sleep, nor is it something that is developed over night. Osmosis will not work for this character [God-like] trait. We must have a self-restraint in our minds before it becomes evident in our actions.

I am a nurse by profession. I spent three years [initially] in college preparing for my career. One year was devoted to pre-requisites, and two years were devoted specifically to the course work needed to complete the necessary requirements to obtain a degree in nursing. At the end of three years I went on to pass the state boards qualifying me to work as a licensed Registered Nurse. I later returned to college in pursuit of a bachelor's degree. The next step will be the master's level, and the final step will be the doctorate level. These advanced level degrees qualify one to teach others the art of Nursing.

As in any other profession, nurses attain different levels of skill with each degree. In the same manner, there is a required number of years training and experience necessary to become a professional [advanced practice] Christian. Based on years of lowliness, meekness, longsuffering, and forbearing, our endurance qualifies us to teach and train others in the body of Christ.

Every two years the state requires that professionals renew their license in order to continue to practice. With each renewal continuing education credits are required. As Christians, we must continue to study as instructed in 2 Timothy 2:15, so that on the day of Christ's appearing we are found "approved". The word of God is the foundation for continuing education materials [instruction] for Christians. In addition we should read Christian books, attend Sunday school and church regularly, and fellowship with other believers in order to continually build ourselves up in the faith.

Here is a list of recommended reading which I have compiled for those of you believing God for a mate. Our main focus should be (of course) getting ourselves right as (single) Christians first and foremost before we begin to focus on the study of being a wife (or husband). Studying to become a professional Christian first [if you will] is our prerequisite to becoming a good wife (or husband).

- Beauty for Ashes by Joyce Meyer (Time Warner Book Group (Fenton, MI) 1994, 2000)
- Even With My Issues by Dr. Wanda Davis-Turner (Whitaker House (New Kensington, PA) 2001)
- Every Young Man's Battle by Stephen Arterburn, Fred Stoeker, & Mike Yorkey Waterbrook Press (a division of Random House, Inc.) (Colorado Springs, CO) 2002)
- Every Young Woman's Battle by Shannon Ethridge & Stephen Arterburn Waterbrook Press (a division of Random House, Inc.) (Colorado Springs, CO) 2004)
- Girl, Get Your Money Straight by Glinda Bridgforth Broadway Books (New York, NY) 2002)
- Girl, Make Your Money Grow by Glinda Bridgforth & Gail Perry-Mason Broadway Books (New York, NY) 2003)
- Let Me Be a Woman by Elisabeth Elliot Tyndale House Publishers, Inc. (Wheaton, ILL) 1976, 2004)
- No More Sheets by Juanita Bynum Pneuma Life Publishing (Lanham, MD) 1998)
- Sassy, Single, & Satisfied by Michelle McKinney Hammond Harvest House Publishers (Eugene, OR) 2003)
- Single, Saved, and Having Sex by Ty Adams Warner Books (West Bloomfield, MI) 2003, 2006)
- Sex Traps by Dr. Wanda Davis-Turner Treasure House (Shippensburg, PA) 1997)
- Teach Me How to Love You by Thomas Weeks, III Legacy Publishers, International (Denver, CO) 2003)
- The Princess Within by Serita Jakes Bethany House Publishers (Bloomington, MN) 1999)

- Woman Thou Art Loosed by Bishop T.D. Jakes Bethany House Publishers (Bloomington, MN) 1996, 2004)

List is limited, and based solely on personal preference

CHAPTER 15

Prepare to be Found

Let us now take a look at some Bible basics (if you will). Throughout Old Testament history, we see that marriage is discouraged between those who are of different cultures and different spiritual backgrounds. Here are just a few scriptures for review: Genesis 24:3; Genesis 28:1; Deuteronomy 7:3; Ezra 9:10-12; and Nehemiah 13:23-27.

II Corinthians 6:14 says that we should not be "unequally yoked together with unbelievers". It continues... "For what fellowship hath righteousness with unrighteousness? And what communion hath light with darkness?" (KJV)

To be unequally yoked means to be different, foreign, or strange. People who are unequally yoked do not speak the same language, do not have the same belief system, and their convictions will be different. Their individual values and standards will be different. If you read the history books, you will see why these unions were discouraged. The doctrines and teachings were different and therefore trouble would usually ensue.

Look at I Kings the 11th chapter. "But King Solomon loved many strange women," (I Kings 11:1a). These women turned Solomon's heart away from God and had him doing things that were dishonorable and detestable. You see, being unequally yoked will have you doing things out of character. It will have you compromising your own beliefs and standards. To be unequally yoked is not God's best for us as Christians.

Now let us take a closer look [ladies especially] at some other scriptures that will help us to 'prepare to be found'. Again, let us look at Proverbs 31. Although some may not believe this is realistic, I [personally] believe that we are Proverbs 31 women already. These qualities are obtainable; we simply need someone to love us unconditionally, and pull the characteristics of this woman out of us. Remember, "...all things are possible to him that believeth." (Mark 9:23b).

Christ has already loved us more completely and unconditionally than any human being we have ever known, or will ever know. So let us begin to walk into our purpose and destiny as women of God first; then when that man whom God has chosen finds us, I believe that we will have already had practice being that Proverbs 31 woman.

Ladies, I am not in any way suggesting that this will be an easy task; but it will come more natural when we get married if we have already been practicing these characteristics while we were single.

Proverbs 18:22 says, "Whoso findeth a wife findeth a good thing, and obtaineth favor of the Lord." (KJV) A wife is supposed to be her husband's 'good thing'-his 'favor'. (Read also Psalm 128:3; Proverbs 12:4; Proverbs 19:14; Ephesians 5:22-24; I Peter 3:1-6; and I Corinthians the entire 7th chapter). There is no substitute for the Word of God. I strongly encourage you, as I said before, to search the scriptures and read as much as you can; not just about marriage, but about being Christ-like.

Matthew 5:13-16 reads "Ye are the salt of the earth; but if the salt have lost his savor, wherewith shall it be salted? It is thenceforth good for nothing, but to be cast out, and to be trodden under foot of men. Ye are the light of the world. A city that is set on a hill cannot be hid. Neither do men light a candle, and put it under a bushel, but on a candlestick; and it giveth light unto all that are in the house. Let your light so shine before men, that they may see your good works, and glorify your Father which is in heaven." As Christian women, we must keep in mind that before we think about being someone's wife, we must first and foremost be 'salt and light' to the world.

God will not let a man find us until He is sure that we are *ready* to be found. In the meantime, we must continue to study to show ourselves approved. We must continue to be busy in our local churches; we must continue to work on getting our finances together. We must continue to focus on Christ.

CHAPTER 16

Now That I'm Found

Now I would be remiss if I simply stated to you reasons not to get married, and did not share with you healthy reasons to consider marriage. I must also add that counseling is an absolute necessity. I discourage anyone from even considering marriage without some sort of pre-marital counseling.

You will find that different ministries have different requirements for pre-marital counseling. One ministry may have a marriage ministry class whereas another may not; your Pastor may require three months, and another may require six months. If your church does not have a *structured* pre-marital counseling program, I advise you to seek out professionals in the Christian arena; your counseling *should* be Bible based.

When it comes to finances, it should not matter how much this counseling cost. Do be mindful to 'comparatively shop' (for lack of better terms), however, this is a necessity and should be a priority. I consider pre-marital counseling to be an investment into our futures. Some reasons to consider marriage are: ministry, companionship, and/or to fulfill sexual needs God's way. We must be convinced that it is God's will for us to marry, and that this person is the individual who God is calling us to spend the rest of our lives with [until death do us part]. We must also be certain that this is the right 'season' for us to marry.

In addition to the fruit of the Spirit (cf. Galatians 5:22-23), some other *marriage-ability* traits include: adaptability and flexibility, empathy, emotional stability, communication skills, ability to work through problems, similarities between the couple (similar likes, dislikes, hobbies, habits, family backgrounds), and the ability to give and receive love.[10] The reason I say 'give and receive love' is because some may feel that they do not deserve to be loved because of past faults and failures (especially failed relationships and/or marriages).

Before attempting to be a husband or wife, sometimes individuals must learn to love *healthy*. Because of childhood and/or past family issues, 'love' must be practiced. 'Real love' may be hindered due to deep seeded issues that must come to the surface and be dealt with. This is another reason why pre-marital counseling is so important. Some issues may be buried so deeply that we may not know that they are still issues [in our lives].

Good communication is also very important; though very important, it is not an easy. Communication is something that must be practiced in order to be mastered. As a woman thinks, feels, perceives, acts, and reacts, is totally foreign to men; so is the way men think, feel, perceive, act, and react foreign to women.

Fellowship is also a very important thing. Women, do not be tricked because the man *says* he is saved. Fellowship with him; continue to fast and pray. Only time and discernment will reveal whether he *really* loves the Lord, or if he is just trying to trap you. Both individuals should have fellowship on an individual level as

---

10 Wright, H. Norman "So You're Getting Married (The Keys to Building a Strong, Lasting Relationship)"

well as on a corporate level.

Ladies, in your considering if this is truly the man that God has ordained for you to marry, question if he can bring you a reference from his Pastor (if you both do not fellowship at the same church). Does he know the word of God? Does he have a prayer life? Can you see the fruit of the Spirit in his life? Don't be tricked ladies. If you think that you have heard from God and then months later realize that your discernment may have been off, back up; slow down. Sure he may be the one, but this may not be the season. Give God some time to continue to work on both of you.

Colossians 4:6 tells us "Let your speech be always with grace, seasoned with salt, that ye may know how ye ought to answer every man." A husband's words ought to be seasoned so that the wife is ministered to every time he speaks. Every hurt, every issue, should be healed by the words that come out of his mouth. It is one thing for a woman to go to church and receive a word from the Pastor, but the word that she receives from her husband [her prophet, priest, and king] should reach places that no other man (or woman), Pastor (or otherwise) can reach.

In knowing that this is the person that God has ordained for us to spend the rest of our lives with, we must consider our conversations. Does the individual build us up or tear us down? We have already been involved in enough damaging relationships; it is time for us to be built up only and not torn down.

Think for a moment of the vows repeated during a wedding ceremony: for better or for worse, for richer or for poorer, in sickness and in health, forsaking all others as long as you both shall live. If we are not ready, willing, and able to forsake everyone and everything for another person then we are not ready to be married. Webster's defines forsake as '...to quit or leave entirely; abandon; desert; to give up or renounce; to deny; to reject'.

The Word of God speaks of becoming one flesh (Gen 2:24). When we truly take on that concept there is no way that we can let anyone or anything come between us. Think of it this way: our bodies have bones, and covering those bones are muscles, tissues, and skin. There is no way that we can separate our skin, tissues, or muscles from our bones without causing severe damage or even death. As well, there should be nothing and no one who can separate us from our spouses [for any reason] barring death. Are we truly ready for that, ladies? Are we *really* ready to say "I do"?

No matter what we have been through in life, we must believe that we are worthy of receiving God's love through another human being. There is a man of God who has been tailor made for each of us; the Lord has sculpted, prepared and made him to fit us precisely.

"Behold ye among the heathen, and regard, and wonder marvelously: for I will work a work in your days, which ye will not believe, though it be told you." Habakkuk 1:5

We have received our prophecies; we perceive in our spirits that this is the man that God has ordained for us. We have prepared ourselves to be found; and now our Boaz' have come.

Rejoice in the God of your salvation, who has counted you worthy to be found.

"But I found him whom my soul loveth: I held him, and would not let him go" Song of Solomon 3:4

"Amazing grace how sweet the sound that saved a wretch like me; I once was lost but now am found was blind but now I see."

REFERENCES

- Angels A to Z. (1996). Lewis, J.R., Oliver, E.D. Detroit, MI: Visible Ink Press
- Don't Call it Love. (1992). Carnes, Patrick, PhD. New York: Bantam Books
- Jones and Bartlett Publishers, LLC. (2009). from www.jbpub.com
- Prayers That Avail Much. (1997). Word Ministries, Inc. Tulsa, OK: Harrison House, Inc.
- Random House Webster's College Dictionary. (1992). New York: Random House
- So You're Getting Married (The Keys to Building a Strong, Lasting Relationship). Wright, H. Norman. Richardson, Texas: Grace Products Corporation
- The Hebrew Greek Key Study Bible. (1991). Chattanooga, TN: AMG International, Inc.
- The New Strong's Complete Dictionary of Bible Words. (1996). Nashville, TN: Thomas Nelson Publishers
- The Revised Standard Version. (1962). Cleveland, OH: The World Publishing Company
- The Thompson Chain-Reference Bible. (1988). Indianapolis, IN: B.B. Kirkbride Bible Co., Inc.
- Today's New International Version. (2005). Grand Rapids, MI: Zondervan

Elder Velva J. Rainey, Co-Pastor

Elder Velva J. Rainey is the Co-Pastor of New Antioch Full Gospel Baptist Church in Newark, Delaware. Her husband of twenty-six years, Rev. Dr. Mark W. Rainey, Sr., is the Founder and Pastor of this body of spirit-filled believers where the five-fold ministries of God are in operation. Along with Pastor Rainey, Co-Pastor Rainey ministers to the needs of New Antioch through the preached and taught Word of God. She also utilizes her teaching gift to impart knowledge through the Genesis New Member's training curriculum. Her passion for the gospel is displayed through the genuine love she has for seeing New Antioch's sheep grow in the things of God. Co-Pastor Rainey's ministry also includes being the Facilitator of the Sisters of Light Women's Ministry. Through this dynamic ministry she provides spiritual leadership and guidance to women who desire a closer relationship with Christ. Her ministry to women and married couples has blossomed the gift to author two books as led by the Holy Spirit "Maintaining a Christian Marriage - Helpful Hints for the Christian Wife", and "The Life Nobody Wants, A Life Without Love". Co-Pastor Velva J. Rainey simply desires to please God and prays that God's women will know the power they have through Him to possess spiritually rich lives.

ABOUT THE AUTHOR

Erlease Freeman was born and raised in the power of the Church. Multiple encounters with the enemy left her battered, bruised, and on a roller-coaster ride destined for an eternal Hell. Her cry (like that of the Samaritan Woman) was "...Lord, give me this living water..." (St. John 4:15). Now refreshed by the fire of the Holy Spirit, she has a passion to minister to hurting girls and woman everywhere. She has surrendered her life to God and committed herself to serving the Body of Christ 'as unto the Lord'. Her first book 'El Shaddai: God My Sufficiency' (Rivers of Living Water Publishing Co., LLC) was released in 2007. She is the mother of one and resides in Greenville, Delaware. She serves under Dr. Christopher Alan Bullock at the Canaan Baptist Church in New Castle, Delaware.

www.ingramcontent.com/pod-product-compliance
Lightning Source LLC
Chambersburg PA
CBHW031300290426
44109CB00012B/654